The Wit and Wisdom of Donald Trump

SKYSCRAPER PUBLICATIONS

"No US President has ever shown this level of intelligence, sophistication and wit. America should appreciate the significance of its decision on November 8th 2016."

The Publisher

Contents

Introduction   1

How I would bring peace to the world   3

How I would heal the divisions in American
society between racial, ethnic and lifestyle groups   15

How I will protect the rights of women   27

How I will demonstrate restraint, civilised
behavior, and compassion   39

The major positive achievements of my business career   51

Tributes from the major beneficiaries of my
charitable giving   63

The major benefits my presidency will bring to
the USA   75

Testimonials to my good qualities from
leading statesmen   87

Acknowledgments   105

Introduction

Those people who were horrified by the election of Donald
Trump to the US presidency clearly had no true idea of the
nature of this man's mind. They judged him solely by his
remarks during the campaign, remarks crafted – sometimes
with the help of others – to appeal to US voters with crisp one-
liners that were designed to convey a philosophy of govern-
ment which many Americans craved. But the true mind of
Donald Trump is different. As this book shows, a team of
researchers scouring everything that Trump has written has
come up with a surprising result. Anyone who looks at the fol-
lowing pages under the various headings that highlight what
people want to know about Trump will come away with a new
appreciation of America's 45th president. Trump is far from
being a caricature of bigotry, male chauvinism and racism.
That characterisation would imply a degree of thought and
consideration of the issues which is entirely absent from the
mind of Donald Trump. As the exhaustive research for this
book has shown, there is nothing at all in Donald Trump's
brain, apart from a few basic human – or perhaps animal –
impulses; an ego the size of one of his gimcrack hotels; and a
depth of ignorance of statesmanship deeper than the Marianas
Trench. Where the actions of past US presidents have been
driven by carefully considered policies, intelligent assimilation
of information, and skills in human relations, this new era will
start with a blank slate, which can be taken as a metaphorical
representation of Trump's mind.

No one reading this book can be in any doubt that Donald
Trump's presidency is on course to go down in history as the
most egregious in the 240 years of United States history.

How I would bring peace to the world

How I would heal the divisions in American society between racial, ethnic and lifestyle groups

How I will protect the rights of women

How I will demonstrate restraint, civilised behavior, and compassion

The major positive achievements of my business career

Tributes from the
major beneficiaries of my
charitable giving

The major benefits my presidency will bring to the USA

Testimonials to my good qualities from leading statesmen

Acknowledgments

Our thanks go first to Donald Trump, without whose startling absence of original thought, compassion, logic or humanity this book would not have been possible.

Second, we would like to thank those voters whose credulity put Donald Trump in the White House, thwarting a political process which the Founding Fathers of the United States of America designed so as to put statesmen rather than buffoons in the role of president.